Let's Discuss

ENERGY RESOURCES

Wind Power

Richard and Louise Spilsbury

PowerKiDS
press.
New York

Published in 2012 by
The Rosen Publishing Group Inc.
29 East 21st Street,
New York, NY 10010

First Edition

Editorial Director: Rasha Elsaeed
Produced for Wayland by Discovery Books Ltd
Managing Editor: Rachel Tisdale
Designer: Ian Winton
Illustrator: Stefan Chabluk
Picture Researcher: Tom Humphrey

Library of Congress Cataloging-in-Publication Data

Spilsbury, Richard, 1963-
Wind power / by Richard Spilsbury and Louise Spilsbury. – 1st ed.
     p. cm. – (Let's discuss energy resources)
Includes index.
ISBN 978-1-4488-5264-2 (library binding)
1. Wind power–Juvenile literature. I. Spilsbury, Louise. II. Title. III. Series.

TJ820.S65 2012
333.9'2–dc22

2010046940

Photographs:
BP: p. 12; Construction Photography: p. 16 (Imagebroker), p. 21; FEMA: p. 24 (Andrea Booher);
Getty Images: p. 6 (Sean Gallup), p. 22 (Insa Korth/AFP); Istockphoto.com: p. 17 (Rick Rhay);
Newscast: p. 15 (E-On); PPM Energy: p. 13; Practical Action: p. 11; RE Power: p. 14, p. 18,
p. 19, p. 23; Shutterstock: cover (TebNad), p. 5 (TW van Urk), p. 9 (Joop Snijder Jr), p. 10
(Orhan Cam), p. 20 (Borislav Borisov), p. 27; Sky Wind Power Corporation: p. 29 bottom
(Professor Roberts); Statoil Hydro: p. 28; Stormblade: p. 29 top; Wikimedia Commons:
p. 26 (Tuey/Flickr).

Manufactured in China
CPSIA Compliance Information: Batch #WAS1102PK: For Further Information
contact Rosen Publishing, New York, New York at 1-800-237-9932

Contents

The words in **bold** can be found in the glossary on page 31.

Wind Power as an Energy Resource

Every day, in many different ways, energy resources help us to do countless tasks. An engine burns fuel to turn the wheels of a car. Wind in a sail can push a yacht through water. From huge machines in factories to the smallest cell phones, all kinds of devices use electricity made from energy resources.

Renewable and Nonrenewable Energy Resources

Most of the energy we use for electricity—around two-thirds—comes from **fossil fuels**. These fuels include coal, gas, and oil, all of which took millions of years to form underground. Demand for fossil fuels is growing partly because more people around the world are using more and more electricity. When the world's supply of fossil fuels is used up, it cannot be replaced, so these energy resources are known as "nonrenewable."

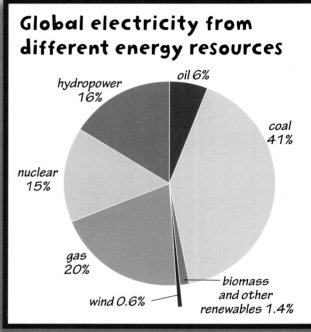

Global electricity from different energy resources

- oil 6%
- coal 41%
- hydropower 16%
- nuclear 15%
- gas 20%
- wind 0.6%
- biomass and other renewables 1.4%

Scientists think all fossil fuels could run out in the next 200 years, so it is important to develop other, renewable sources of energy. Resources such as sunlight, wind, and moving water are renewable—we can use their energy without using them up.

Wind power around the world

- ⑨ Denmark
- ⑧ UK
- ② Germany
- ⑦ France
- ⑩ Portugal
- ① USA
- ③ Spain
- ⑥ Italy
- ④ China
- ⑤ India

This map shows the top 10 producers of electricity using wind power in 2008. The U.S. produced most wind power followed by Germany, Spain, and China.

Why discuss wind power?

In this book, we are going to discuss how we use the wind's energy to produce electricity. There is enough wind energy available on Earth to make five times the power used by everyone across the globe! Today we only use a tiny bit of that energy, but there are some amazing possibilities for wind power in the future.

Global Warming

When fossil fuels are burned for energy, they release carbon dioxide. This is one type of **greenhouse gas** that builds up in the **atmosphere**, storing and trapping heat. Global warming is the overall increase in temperature that greenhouse gases are causing.

Most scientists believe that the extra heat is changing the world's weather patterns, or climate, faster than in the past. Warmer temperatures are melting ice in the Arctic and Antarctica. Other areas are suffering from droughts or extreme storms and flooding. Using renewable forms of energy, such as wind power, to replace fossil fuels will help slow global warming.

Wind farms are groups of wind **turbines** that produce electricity. In the future, there will be more wind farms like this one built at sea.

Capturing the Wind

Where does the wind come from? It all starts with energy from the Sun. The Sun's energy, in the form of heat, warms the Earth's atmosphere. As the air warms, its **molecules** spread out and it gets lighter, so it rises. Cold air is denser, sinks, and pushes out air below it. This air moves into spaces left by rising air. The moving air is wind. The heat energy from the Sun has changed into movement or **kinetic** energy in the wind.

Catching Wind Energy

You probably have felt the kinetic energy in the wind while walking outside on windy days or while flying a kite. To capture that energy, you need the right equipment. Like the sails on a yacht, the blades on a wind turbine catch the wind. The blades are angled and shaped so that when wind blows against them, the blades turn.

The blades and the hub that holds them are called the **rotor**. The rotor is mounted at the top of a tower on a case called the **nacelle**. As it turns, the rotor spins a shaft inside the nacelle. This shaft is connected to a gearbox with cogs inside that make a second shaft spin even faster. The second shaft turns a **generator**.

gearbox

nacelle

shaft

hub

tower

blade

These men are repairing a wind turbine. Lifting the lid of the nacelle shows the gearbox and shaft inside. The generator is in the section at the back.

Which type of turbine works best?

The commonest wind turbines usually have three blades that spin on the nacelle at the top of a tower. These are horizontal axis turbines. The other kind is the vertical axis turbine with several narrow, curved blades that spin around a vertical pole. Each design has its advantages and disadvantages.

Advantages:

Horizontal
The largest turbines have giant blades that can catch lots of wind, at a range of wind speeds, and generate lots of electricity high above the ground.

Vertical
They work even if the wind changes direction and are easier to maintain at ground level.

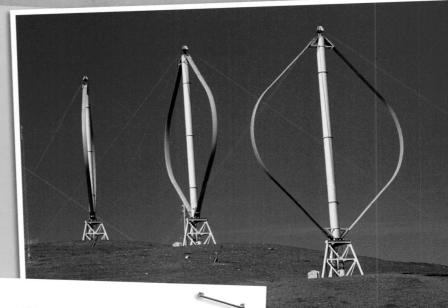

Wires keep these vertical axis turbines upright as their long blades spin.

Disadvantages:

Horizontal
Rotors cannot work if they are not facing the wind or if the wind is too slow.

Vertical
Rotors have a small area to catch wind, and wind is always slower at ground level.

Horizontal turbines are the best for generating lots of electricity, because they have a much bigger size to catch more wind energy.

From Energy to Electricity

We've seen how the kinetic energy of the wind is captured by the wind turbine's rotor. It is converted into mechanical energy when it is used to turn shafts. We cannot use this mechanical energy to run our electrical machines. We have to change it into electrical energy.

The Generator

The rotation of the shafts turns a machine called a generator. It is this generator that produces electricity by converting mechanical energy into electrical energy. Coils of wire move fast within a circle of magnets inside the generator to generate electricity.

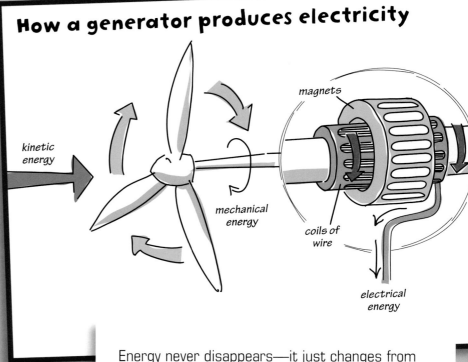

How a generator produces electricity

kinetic energy

mechanical energy

magnets

coils of wire

electrical energy

Energy never disappears—it just changes from one form to another. This diagram shows how a generator produces electricity from wind energy.

Energy and Power

Energy is often described as the ability to do work. You need energy for your body to function. An electric heater needs energy to heat your home. Your body gets its energy from food, while the heater gets its energy from electricity. Energy can be measured in units called joules.

People often use the word "power" to mean a supply of electricity. But power is also the rate at which energy is used or sent. It is measured in units called **watts**, which are joules per second. A 60-watt bulb needs 60 joules of energy each second to make it light up. A kilowatt (kW) is 1,000 watts and a megawatt (MW) is 1 million watts.

We measure the electricity a home or business or whole town consumes in larger units: the kilowatt hour or megawatt hour (kWh or MWh). Over a whole year, the average amount of electricity consumed each hour varies between countries. The highest in 2005 was 28 MWh in Iceland and the lowest 36 kWh in Ethiopia.

Before electricity, windmills converted wind into mechanical energy that farmers used to pump water or grind grain.

Let's Discuss

Wind vs. fossil fuel power.

Advantages:

No Fuel
Wind turbines do not need fossil fuels to keep them turning and generating electricity. They release no greenhouse gases while converting energy.

Efficient Energy Conversion
Wind power converts about two-thirds of the energy in wind into electricity. This is twice the conversion **efficiency** of coal, a fossil fuel.

Disadvantages:

Electricity and Space
Wind farms make 200 times less electricity per square mile of land than a fossil fuel power plant.

Less Wind, Less Power
Few wind turbines make as many kilowatts as they could because the wind does not always blow.

In the right conditions, a wind farm will be cleaner and more efficient than a fossil fuel plant, but take up more space to generate its power.

How People Use Wind Power

Many wind turbines around the world make sufficient electricity for families, businesses and small communities to use. Generating to meet their own needs is called **microgeneration**.

Power without Household Electricity

We take it for granted that refrigerators, TVs, and lights all run off **household electricity**. Around one-quarter of the world's population has no electricity supply. This is usually because the **grid** (the network of cables carrying electricity from power plants) does not reach to where they live. Even in some places that do have a grid, such as Kathmandu in Nepal, power cuts are very common, so people don't have electricity all of the time. Wind turbines are ideal for people who live in windy places with poor access to an electricity supply, from remote mountains of Scotland to Caribbean islands.

Locations

Microgeneration can be used in many locations. Small wind turbines on the tops of vans or yachts, with rotors 3 feet (about 1 meter) wide, can power a few lights. A turbine making enough power for a whole house may need a rotor five times wider than that. Buildings with turbines for microgeneration range from farms in the countryside to tall office buildings in cities.

The three wind turbines on the World Trade Center in Bahrain microgenerate 10–15 percent of the electricity consumed inside the building.

CASE STUDY

Light in Sri Lanka

In Sri Lanka, in south Asia, almost three-quarters of the people live in the countryside and have no access to electricity from the country's power grid. For light, many use oil lamps, which easily cause fires. Other people use old car **batteries** to run light bulbs. This is safer but it is expensive to get the batteries recharged.

The organization Practical Action is working with Sri Lankan villagers to build wind turbines so they can recharge their own batteries. The villagers make the turbines from local materials and maintain the machines themselves. Many villagers now have a free, renewable source of light in which to work, cook, and study.

"It was wonderful! Straight away there was enough power to light a few light bulbs, so I could work and the children could do their homework."

Weerasinghe, Usgala village, Sri Lanka, 2009, after getting a wind turbine.

With free wind power in their village, more families can afford to send their children to school.

Wind Farms on Land

A wind farm is a group of large wind turbines that together generate lots of electricity from one site. The electricity from each turbine feeds into the grid, which distributes this power, along with electricity generated using different energy resources, to large numbers of consumers.

Working Together

An average big turbine on a wind farm can usually generate about 3,000 MWh of electricity. If an average person from the United States uses electricity at a rate of about 6 MWh throughout a year, this turbine supplies enough electricity for about 500 people. Ten turbines together would make enough electricity for about 5,000 people. A site where many turbines are built together can supply a large town.

Putting many turbines up in the same place saves money compared with building turbines separately. The electricity generated by each wind turbine can be carried from one site through cables into the grid. If more electricity is needed, turbines can be added on nearby land.

Construction workers need powerful machinery such as cranes to put up the towers, nacelles, and blades of large turbines on a wind farm.

Spacing

Wind farms need a lot of space. In general only 15 turbines are built on one square mile of land. If turbines are too close behind others, they can block the supply of wind to their neighbors. Therefore, turbines are positioned with more space in front and behind than at the sides. Another reason for spacing out turbines is that a spinning rotor can make air swirl around its edges. The swirling affects the wind so it does not turn other blades nearby as well.

Spacing out turbines across a wind farm makes sure that each generates as much electricity as possible from the farm site.

CASE STUDY

Biggest Wind Farm in Europe

The Whitelee wind farm on Eaglesham Moor, south of Glasgow in Scotland, opened in May 2009. It is the biggest wind farm on European land. It has 140 turbines over an area of 21 square miles (55 square kilometers)—the size of the island of Bermuda. Each turbine can generate 2.3 MW. The predicted power of all the turbines put together is 900,000 MWh a year. An average coal power plant burns about 1 ton of coal to make 1 MWh of electricity, so Whitelee wind farm is saving about 900,000 tons of coal per year. It is also preventing 600,000 tons of carbon dioxide from entering the atmosphere each year.

Spoiling the View

Winds blow slower near the surface of land because there are usually more obstacles, such as trees or buildings, to slow them down. In addition, the **air pressure** drops at higher altitudes because there is less weight of air in the atmosphere pressing downward. Winds can blow faster when there is less air pressure. At 262 feet (80 meters) above the ground, the force of wind is more than twice that at 33 feet (10 meters) above the ground.

Tall Turbines

Wind turbine towers need to be tall, therefore, to catch more wind. The nacelles of many modern turbines are 262 feet (80 meters) high. They are also placed on hills, where the land is open and the wind is stronger. The trouble with this is that some turbines and wind farms can be seen from all around. Many people think they spoil the view in beautiful places.

Wind turbines tower over some hillsides. Do you think they are a blot on the landscape or a symbol of hope in the battle to slow global warming?

"[Wind farms] are a lot less ugly than climate change..."

Environmentalist George Monbiot, the *Guardian* newspaper, UK, 2005

Changing Landscape

Other people argue that wind farms are an acceptable price to pay for cleaner power, even if they do change the landscape. Putting up turbines is one of several human activities that have changed hills over the centuries. These include clearing forests to make fields, mining rocks for building, and making networks of electricity pylons and telephone lines across hills.

Should power companies build wind farms on hills?

Yes:

Wind Farms Attract Tourists

Tourists visit hills to see wind farms and learn about renewable energy resources. They also spend money in other businesses, such as shops, restaurants, and hotels.

Wind Farms Use Spare Land

In many countries, few people live on hillsides. Not too many residents are affected, so wind farms on hills are a good use of land.

Unlike other kinds of power plants, wind farms do not prevent other land use, such as farming.

No:

Turbines Stand Out

Many of the hilly areas where wind is strongest are areas of natural beauty, and some are next to protected land such as national parks. Wind farms change the appearance of the countryside and spoil views for visitors and people who live there.

Wind Farms Affect Communities

Prices of houses and the value of land may drop next to wind farms, because people do not want to live or work nearby. Fewer visitors and residents spend less in local businesses.

It is better to build wind farms where land is less used and has stronger winds than other sites, but we also need to preserve the look of the countryside where possible.

How Wind Farms Affect Health

Wind farms make electricity without greenhouse gases so wind power is healthy for the Earth. However, some people argue that the turbines might be unhealthy for those living close by.

Machine Noise

Some of the mechanical energy in wind turbines gets converted into noise energy. There is a low swishing or thumping noise when the giant blades move through the air. There is also a high humming or whining noise caused by cogs in the gearbox moving against each other. People living near turbines say that all the noise from turbines affects their health. Some hear ringing in their ears all the time. Others feel sick and dizzy or get headaches.

The health effects some homeowners report that turbines cause are one reason people may protest against building new wind farms near where they live.

CASE STUDY

Losing Sleep in Canada

Protest groups campaign against wind farms partly because of their health effects. In Canada, the Wind Concerns Ontario group is concerned about how noise and vibrations from turbines affect sleep. When people do not get enough sleep, they are tired, irritable, and cannot concentrate. The group is trying to make the Canadian government change laws so that wind farms have to be at least 1.25 miles (2 kilometers) away from communities.

"These [wind turbines make it] sound literally like this house is in a washing machine." Barbara Ashbee, Ontario, Canada, talking about turbines near her home.

Blocking the Light

Moving turbine blades can create a long, flickering shadow if sunlight shines low behind them. People who live in the shadow say the flickering is like a powerful flashing light called a strobe.

Let's Discuss

Are wind turbines bad for our health?

Yes:

Constant Irritation
The noise turbines make is continuous, and the health problems they cause can build up.

Serious Problems
Turbines can trigger serious heart and brain problems as well as headaches and dizziness.

The strobe effect of shadows from wind turbines can make some people feel sick and dizzy.

No:

Quiet in Comparison
Turbines are quiet compared with other sound sources, such as traffic. Wind power companies rarely install turbines closer than 1,150 feet (350 meters) to houses. At this distance, they say, the sound is similar to a refrigerator.

Clean Air
Wind turbines make no pollution, and the pollution released by building turbines and setting up wind farms is far less than that from power plants burning fossil fuel.

On balance, far fewer people have their health affected by wind turbines than by the effects of using fossil fuel power.

Wind Farms at Sea

One way to avoid the problems of building wind farms on land is to build them at sea. Winds are stronger along coasts and out at sea because there are fewer obstacles than on land. This means offshore wind farms can generate a lot of electricity.

Building in the Ocean

The sea can be a rough place to put up turbines, however. Waves could knock down the turbines unless they have very firm bases on the sea floor. Many offshore turbine towers have hollow steel bases. The base is dropped to the sea floor and filled with heavy gravel or concrete to weigh it down. The turbine tower is firmly attached to the base. Waves get stronger in deeper water, so offshore wind farms are usually built in water less than 100 feet (30 meters) deep.

It takes a lot of work and money to put up offshore turbines. Therefore, power companies put up the biggest turbines available for offshore locations so that each can generate as much electricity as possible.

Powerful tugboats pull parts of wind turbines out to sea on giant barges. The four vertical legs of the barge are dropped to the sea floor. This keeps the barge stable when its crane lifts the turbine parts into position.

Ocean vs. land turbines.

Advantages:

More Space
There is more space at sea than on land. Wind farms are far enough from people to avoid health problems. Turbines can be huge since there is more space for them to rotate.

Stronger, Lower Wind
Winds blow harder at sea, even at surface level. Turbines at sea can be shorter than those on land and still capture more wind energy.

Disadvantages:

Expensive to Build
Building turbines at sea is much more expensive than on land. It is also very costly to lay power cables to carry electricity to the shore.

Busy Waters
Currently, offshore wind farms are built only in coastal waters. These waters are used by many ships and boats, so turbines can get in the way and be a hazard.

Although more expensive, it is preferable to build wind farms at sea.

This giant offshore wind turbine has a rotor measuring over 394 ft. (120 m) across, and can generate up to 5MW—that's enough for around 1,500 people in the U.S. but many more in countries where people use less electricity.

How Wind Power Affects Wildlife

Moving turbine blades are heavy and sharp, and their tips can reach speeds of over 125 miles (200 kilometers) per hour in very strong winds. No wonder they are a possible danger to some flying animals.

Chopping Blades

Every year, turbine blades kill many bats and birds, including cranes, storks, vultures, and eagles. Lights on tall turbine towers warn airplanes to keep clear, but unfortunately, they may attract tired birds looking for a resting place. Wind farm owners and makers, however, say that most birds avoid the blades. A 2006 Danish study found that few seabirds collided with offshore turbines since they mostly fly low over the sea surface.

Many scientists say that far more birds are killed by cats, in road accidents, or by flying into windows than by hitting turbine blades.

CASE STUDY — Prairie Threat

Prairie land in the United States is a rich mix of tall grasses and other plants. Tall-grass prairie lands are home to threatened animals such as the greater **prairie** chicken. Over 95 percent of the U.S. prairie has been dug up over the years and turned into farmland. One of the last unspoiled areas of prairie, in the Flint Hills, Kansas, is the site of a proposed wind farm of 1,000 turbines, each taller than the Statue of Liberty. Building work will damage plant roots and disturb animals. Some local people say the prairie should not be destroyed for these wind turbines, which would generate just one-tenth of 1 percent of all the electricity used in the U.S.

Do wind turbines harm wildlife?

No:

Less Climate Change
When people use wind power, they help to slow global warming. Most scientists agree that global warming has major adverse effects on enormous numbers of people and wildlife.

Living Space
The bases of turbines at sea provide habitat for shellfish and seaweeds. Fish also feed and breed in the shelter of these spaces.

Yes:

Deadly Power
Birds are killed when they fly into or are electrocuted by power lines from turbine generators. However, birds are in danger from all power lines and power plants.

The movement of heavy machines used to create wind farms on land presses down on soil and damages plants.

Habitat Destruction
Building turbines on land and at sea can destroy habitats that may take a long time to recover. Only then can some living things return.

By slowing global warming, wind turbines harm many fewer animals and plants than they directly affect through damage to land or turbine impacts.

Turbine Safety

Turbine blades are designed to be flexible so they can bend and twist in strong winds. However, powerful winds can make blades split or snap off. The wind can even blow over whole turbines. This has happened in Germany, the United States, the UK, and Denmark.

Weather Effects

In cold places, snow and ice can collect on turbine blades. Spinning rotors can throw big chunks of ice hundreds of yards from turbines. Of course, extreme weather can affect the safety of all kinds of power supply structures, not just turbines.

Testing Blades

Before they are installed, turbine blades are tested for strength. One end of a test blade is clamped to a giant concrete block, and then a machine makes it bend thousands of times. This process tests how strong winds would affect blades over many years. During the test, other machines check materials in the blade. They can show where the blade is heating up because of materials pulling apart. If the layers pulled apart on a working blade, it might shred, break, and fall to the ground.

A falling blade weighing many tons can damage anything it lands on. But turbine accidents affect much smaller areas than problems with **nuclear power** plants, for instance.

Looking After Turbines

Maintenance workers inspect turbines regularly to see if they are working properly. For example, they check for worn-out parts in the gearboxes and for cracks in blades. Maintenance is expensive, partly because work in nacelles high above the ground is dangerous. But it is cheaper and safer than allowing the turbine to break down or cause an accident.

Workers maintaining tall wind turbines wear safety harnesses so they cannot fall. However, since 1990, more than 20 workers have been injured in accidents while maintaining wind turbines.

Let's Discuss

Wind turbines are a safe way to generate electricity.

Advantages:

Safety Features
Turbines have brakes to slow rotors in high winds. **Sensors** can detect strong vibrations in rotors and automatically turn them off.

Safe Power
Wind power has a better safety record than many other kinds of power. For example, thousands of coal miners die each year in mining accidents in China.

Disadvantages:

Real Stresses
The stresses of extreme weather are much greater than those in tests. They can make blades break and cause safety features, such as brakes and sensors, to fail.

Fire Risk
Gearboxes can overheat and start fires in the nacelle. These are difficult to put out because normal firefighting equipment cannot reach the flames.

Using wind turbines creates safety risks, but wind power is much safer than many other power technologies.

Wind Supply and Demand

Winds blow at different speeds around the world and at different times of the day or year. This means that wind power can not always supply enough electricity to meet global demand.

Where the Wind Blows

The strength of winds in the world's **temperate** zones are affected by the rotation of the Earth relative to the Sun. Generally, in temperate places such as Scandinavia, the northwestern United States, or New Zealand, winds are stronger by day than at night and in winter than in summer. This is because these are the times when temperate places are slightly closer to the Sun. In Denmark, there is usually plenty of wind to meet demand for heating and light in the colder, darker winter months. But in warm summers in the United States, there may not be enough wind power to operate air-conditioners.

Global warming could change wind patterns and increase the number of extreme weather events, such as this hurricane in New Orleans. Changing winds may cause future problems for wind farms.

Stopping Turbines

Even in the windiest places, such as Antarctica, winds do not blow all of the time. Wind turbines stop generating when the wind does not blow. Large turbines can generate some power in wind as slow as 9.3 miles (15 kilometers) per hour, but their maximum power generated is in winds of about 62 miles (100 kilometers) per hour. Turbines also stop when wind speeds get too high. Power companies turn them off because the winds may damage their machines.

Meeting Demand

When there is not enough wind power because turbines are not turning, power companies need to use other energy resources. They often have to burn fossil fuels to generate the electricity that consumers demand. At times when there is more wind energy than people need, however, it can be stored to meet demand on still days or when people suddenly need lots of electricity. This can happen, for example, when more people than expected watch a football game on TV! Wind power companies usually store wind energy in the form of electrical energy in batteries. They can also store wind energy in compressed air (see below).

CASE STUDY

Wind Power from Caves

Germany makes about 20 percent of the world's wind power, mostly in the windy northern parts of the country. Since 1978, the German town of Huntorf in northern Germany has stored excess electricity from wind power by compressing or pushing air into underground caves.

1. When there is more electricity from wind turbines than people can use, electric pumps push air into the caves. Compressing gives the air potential or stored energy.
2. When people need electricity in a hurry, the power company releases the compressed air.
3. The high-pressure air burns with gas operating a gas turbine more efficiently than burning with uncompressed air. This generates extra electricity to feed into the town's grid.

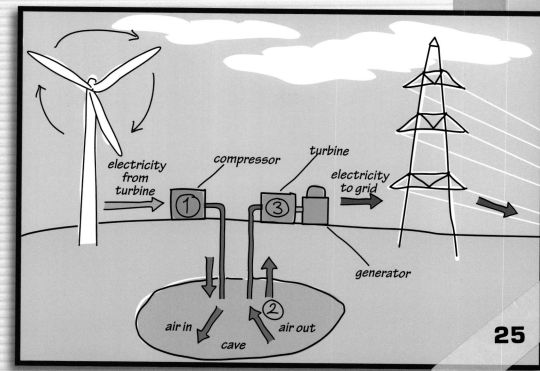

The Cost of Wind Power

For wind power to increase in use around the world, the electricity it generates has to be close in price to that from fossil fuel or nuclear power plants. As for any power technology, the expensive part of wind power is setting up the equipment to generate power. However, wind, like many renewables, has no further costs of fuel.

Starting Up

It costs about $2.7 million to buy and set up a wind turbine that can generate 1 MW. The expenses include buying land, buying machinery, building and installing the machines, and connecting them to the electricity supply. In some countries, companies that start up wind farms can get financial help from their government. Governments **subsidize** wind farms because they have made global agreements to reduce greenhouse gases. For example, the U.S. government pays companies a small amount for every kWh of wind power they generate. Then the companies can supply electricity from wind turbines to consumers that are similar to prices of fossil fuel-generated electricity.

The price of a turbine includes strong but light blades made in specialized facilities, such as this LM Glasfiber factory in North Dakota.

Comparing Prices

With present-day turbine technology, power from wind farms costs an average of around 6 cents per kWh. It is more from offshore wind farms that are more expensive to set up. Wind power is more expensive than nuclear power and fossil fuel power, but it is cheaper than solar and **geothermal** power. **Hydroelectric power** is currently the cheapest renewable energy

Using Less Power

Some people say governments should not just subsidize renewable energy. They should help people use less power by subsidizing ways to save energy. People use a lot of their household power to heat homes. **Insulating** an attic prevents heat escaping through the roof, so less power is needed for heat. A study by a UK insulation company found that insulating the attics of 500 homes saved the total amount of power made by a 750 kW wind turbine each year.

Energy efficient light bulbs last four times as long and use less power than standard ones.

Let's Discuss

Governments should encourage wind turbines.

Advantages:

Helping All Energy Resources
It is fair that governments should subsidize renewable energy, including wind, because they already subsidize fossil fuel and nuclear power industries.

Reducing Cost
Wind power could become cheaper than fossil fuel power if fossil fuel users have to pay for reducing greenhouse and polluting gases.

Disadvantages:

Still Too Expensive
Wind power is more expensive than nonrenewables even with subsidies, so it cannot be the right energy solution.

Not Enough
Wind cannot supply enough power for the planet. Governments are encouraging wind farms in order to reduce greenhouse gases.

Governments should encourage wind power as part of a mix of ways to generate enough electricity while slowing global warming.

The Future for Wind Power

Like all renewable energy resources, wind power will be an important part of the global energy mix in future. As we have discussed, it will work better in some places than others. And certain problems, such as energy storage and health hazards, will have to be addressed.

Looking Ahead

China, the United States, and northern and western Europe will probably expand their wind power faster than other regions because they have good wind energy resources. They also have governments that encourage the use of wind power. China expects to be generating twice as much wind power as nuclear power by 2020. Europe could be getting one-tenth of all its power from the wind by 2020.

Out at Sea

Future offshore wind farms will be mostly built far out at sea where winds are strongest. Turbines will have vast blades to capture more energy. New technology will be needed to keep the turbines upright and stable in deep water. Windfloat is a wide floating base for turbines. It has broad paddles and motors that help keep the turbine upright in powerful winds and waves.

Floating turbines have weights in their hollow base to float upright and are anchored to the seafloor using strong chains.

Future Wind Power on Land

Wind power companies predict there will be hundreds of thousands more small turbines on land microgenerating electricity for individuals and companies. We may also see newer designs of wind turbines on future wind farms that are more efficient at capturing wind energy than those of today.

Stormblade is a turbine that looks a little like a jet engine, with its blades inside the nacelle. Its designers say Stormblade's shape funnels wind onto the blades, making it twice as efficient as other turbines at getting energy from the wind. The shape also prevents harm to wildlife.

Stormblade should be able to turn in a wider range of wind speeds than normal turbines, shown here to contrast the shapes.

Power Kites in the Sky

In the future, people could make wind power from the strong and constant winds high in the sky. You may have felt this power when flying a kite on a long string. Flying electric generators look like kites and would be connected to Earth by cables up to 0.6 miles (1 kilometer) long. Their spinning blades would keep them aloft and generate electricity that travels to the ground through the cables.

The flying electric generator would use the most powerful winds on Earth that blow high in the atmosphere.

Wind Activity

Make a Working Turbine

You can make a very simple wind turbine to do the job of weight lifting!

What you need:
- Bottle cork
- Wooden flower stick (about 12 in. (30 cm) long)
- Piece of thin card, trimmed to a square
- Wide straw that the stick will easily turn inside
- Rubber bands and glue
- A house brick
- 20 in. (50 cm) thread
- Hairdryer
- Thumbtack and paper clip
- Small toy

1 Make a pinwheel rotor by cutting the card as in the diagram below. Pin and glue four corners of the card through the center of the pinwheel onto the cork. Push the cork firmly onto the wooden stick.

2 Use the rubber bands to attach the straw to the brick and lie the brick on the edge of a table. Put the stick into the straw so part of the stick nearest the rotor is hanging over the table edge. Make the stick stay in place using rubber bands on either side of the straw, making sure it can still turn.

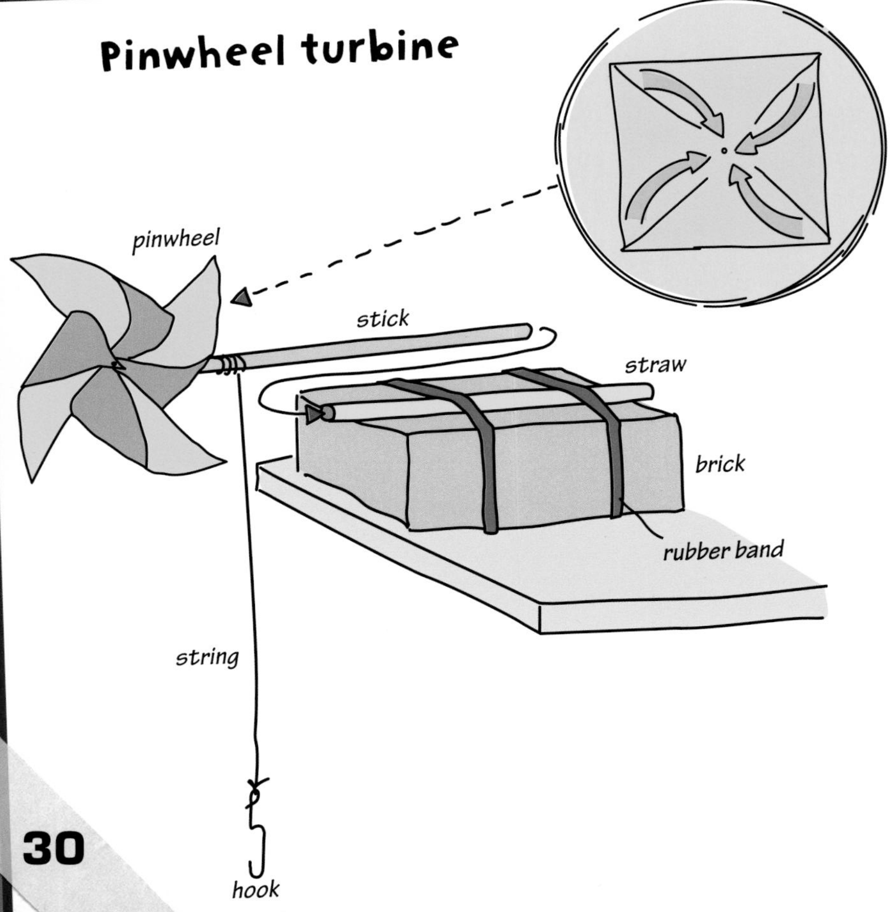

3 Tie one end of the thread on the part of the flower stick just behind the cork. Tie the other end to the paper clip, bent into a hook shape. Attach a small weight such as a toy to the hook.

4 Use the hairdryer to blow onto the rotor to wind up the string. Does it wind up faster if you make the hairdryer blow faster or move it nearer to the rotor? Do you predict that the turbine will need more or less wind power to lift a heavier object?

Pinwheel turbine

pinwheel

stick

straw

brick

rubber band

string

hook

Wind Topics and Glossary

History
- Research a wind power timeline from the earliest windmills in Persia and China up to the present day. When and where was wind power first used to generate electricity?

Geography
- Look at the maps at www.stanford.edu/group/efmh/winds/global_winds.html. These show average wind speeds 80 meters above ground around the world. For each continent, make a list of five good locations for wind farms.

Design and Technology
- Use the Internet to find out about new wind turbine designs. You could search for: Quiet Revolution, Selsam Superturbine, Laddermill, and Magenn Air Rotor. Now use these as inspiration for your own turbine design.

English
- Imagine you live near hills where a power company wants to build a new wind farm. Write a letter to the company giving reasons why they should build the turbines somewhere else.

Science
- Find out why the curved shape of turbine blades creates a sideways force when struck by wind from the front.

Glossary

air pressure push of the atmosphere caused by the weight of air.

atmosphere mix of gases surrounding the Earth up to the edge of space.

battery store of electrical energy.

efficiency when resources, such as energy, are used wisely and not wasted.

fossil fuel fuel such as coal formed over millions of years from remains of living things.

generator machine that converts mechanical into electrical energy.

geothermal natural heat from rocks deep underground.

greenhouse gas gas such as carbon dioxide that traps heat in the atmosphere.

grid system of wires and pylons for sending electricity across a wide area.

household electricity electricity supplied through the grid to consumers.

hydroelectric power generating electricity using moving water from rivers or reservoirs.

insulate use material to prevent loss of heat or other energy.

kinetic produced by movement.

microgeneration small-scale production of electricity to meet the needs of users.

molecule smallest unit of a substance, made of a group of atoms.

nacelle protective covering of the shaft, gearbox, and generator in a wind turbine.

nuclear power energy released by splitting atoms of special metals.

prairie flat, wide grassland area in North America.

rotor hub with blades that rotates on a wind turbine.

sensor device that reacts to changes in wind to control a wind turbine.

subsidize pay to support something and encourage its success.

temperate region with mild temperatures between the equator and the poles.

turbine machine for converting linear into mechanical kinetic energy.

watt measure of power or energy (joules) used per second.

Further Information, Web Sites, and Index

Books

Fueling the Future: Wind Energy
by Elizabeth Raum
(Heinemann Raintree, 2008)

Future Energy: Wind and Water
by Jim Holloff
(Abdo Publishing Company, 2010)

*The World of Energy: Understanding
   Wind Power*
by Polly Goodman
(Gareth Stevens Publishing, 2010)

Web Sites

Due to the changing nature of Internet links, PowerKids Press has developed an online list of Web sites related to the subject of this book. This site is updated regularly. Please use this link to access this list: http://www.powerkidslinks.com/lder/wind/

Index